Unearth the Treasure in Your Child

Nick Nunayon

Published by Soteric Publishers

First published in UK in 2015 by Soteric Publishers

www.kingsgen.co.uk

ISBN Number 978-0-9933001-0-3

Book cover designed by ShalomWales Graphics: admin@kingsgen.co.uk

Since the publication of this book, some of the websites referred to might have changed as a result of technological advancement or for other reasons.

First published in the by Soteric Publishers.

First print July 2015

Second reprint September 2015

Third reprint October 2015

Fourth reprint September 2016

Revised edition June 2017

ENDORSEMENTS

"I enjoyed reading this book and there is some very useful advice for parents here! The fact that you refer to your own children and your own experiences makes it very readable - it is not simply a list of instructions/advice."

Sue Bridger, a former grammar school English teacher, private tutor and parent.

"Your book is very informative and the testimonies say it all how much it is appreciated that you are guiding the parents. I like the way you have written the book and given the facts and information."

Ines Connors, a retired secondary school head of English.

"Well done for putting this book together. The readers will be enlightened by the content."

Idevert Agui, Vice Principal, Walworth Academy,

London.

"This book inspired me and helped me understand the UK education system much better. It has empowered me to know what to do with my children. It will empower parents to know what to do at each educational level with their children and how to support their children."

Valentine Mogaji, ACMA. Financial and Management Consultant, school governor and parent.

"The primary/ secondary school transfer process can be very overwhelming, especially for parents. The author of this book has given valuable insights on how to make the transition process more manageable and less burdensome. If parents can be thorough in taking the suggestions on board together with their children's cooperation then the treasure within the children is bound to emerge forthwith gloriously without hindrance. I have personally tested some of the insights within this book and I know they work. KNOWLEDGE INDEED IS POWER. Well done, Pastor Nick, for sharing these valuable insights."

Mrs. Olusola Goriola, science teacher and parent.

"Most of us, when we receive a gift, treasure it and take good care of it. The Bible tells us that 'children are a heritage from the Lord' so the implications are clear. Good care is an obligation and that has to extend to caring for our children within the education system. Nick Nunayon's book is an inspiring practical resource, packed with relevant information and marked by a well-balanced approach to the individual child's potential and general well-being. He writes as a parent and an educationalist, having a concern that extends beyond his own children to the children of others. I whole-heartedly agree with the parent who commended 'Pastor Nick' for his 'passion, enthusiasm and positive attitude'. I would also commend him for achieving all that he does without putting anyone under undue pressure. This book will enable you to help your child in ways that will continue to bring rewards, both academically and relationally."

Dr. Hugh Osgood, Founder and President, Churches in Communities International, Moderator of Free Churches, UK, President of Churches Together.

"This book is a wealth of information. I wish I had access to this when my children were younger but I am more determined now to ensure I tell as many people who care to listen about this great book.

Pastor Nick's passion is evident in the way the book has been written. He has left no stone unturned, so this must be an 'educational bible' for every home or rather everyone with a vision to see their child(ren) attain greatness. This book has really fuelled my passion to do everything legitimately possible to see my children have a better tomorrow. Thank you, sir, for your guidance!"

Rev. Victoria Lawrence, parent advocate for children with special needs (Kent, UK).

"I came across Pastor Nunayon's book while enquiring about the resources that would help me to encourage, guide, and support my children towards academic excellence. The book is a MUST READ

for every parent who is determined to secure the best education for their children. Pastor Nick's genuine passion and insight to see every child achieve their full potential is to be commended. From how to pass Eleven Plus, SATS, GCSE's and A-levels to how to make an application form to public schools, the book is a manual filled with possibilities for every parent. I admire Pastor Nunayon for his labour of love, and pray that he continues to be a blessing to countless children and parents who are following in his footsteps of academic excellence. God bless you."
Andreja Oshevire.

"This book does precisely what it says - shares priceless, tested, and detailed insights about how to navigate and demystify the daunting maze of the British Educational System. You can gain invaluable nuggets of wisdom from this book, which have taken other people years to acquire, oftentimes making costly mistakes in the process. It will transform the life of your child and set them on the path to achieve their highest potential. My confidence has soared, as the book inspires both the child and the parent to aim for resounding success and, most importantly, shows how to achieve it. I found Pastor Nick's passion for educational excellence incredibly heart-warming and radiating through every page. Thank you Pastor Nick for choosing to be a blessing!!!"

Mrs. Jumoke Erin-Oluwa

DEDICATION

This book is dedicated to God who gave me the opportunity to be a blessing to my generation; to my late parents, Pa and Mrs James Nunayon, who were unable to read and write but did everything in their power to ensure that I received a formal education; and to Oluyemi Nunayon, the love of my life, my friend, confidant, helper, co-labourer, wife, and to our beloved children Agape and Simon, my inspirations.

ACKNOWLEDGEMENTS

I thank God for calling, choosing and anointing me to be His servant, and for inspiring me to impart and impact many lives around me, including the younger generation.

I am grateful to my beloved and wonderful wife for being a source of encouragement and inspiration, and for bringing out the gift of mentoring and coaching in me.

I thank our two children, Agape and Simon, who have been my helpful 'guinea pigs' and willing participants for the testing of all inspired and researched ideas. You are great and blessings to your generation.

I thank my spiritual father and mentor in the ministry, Dr. Hugh Osgood, for his encouragement and prayers, and my adopted senior brother Mr. Felix Bamtefa who was there for me during my secondary school days, always advising me to focus on my education and not to follow the quick ways of making money or to become a teenage father like some of my peers.

My special thanks go to Monsignor Chris Ajala of the Catholic Dioceses of Abeokuta, Nigeria and Professor Emmanuel

Babatunde of the University of Lincoln, USA for their financial support during my HND programme. My appreciation also goes to all of my teachers and lecturers in primary school, secondary school, in polytechnics and universities: thank you for your contribution to my life.

To all my spiritual children, tutees, mentees and friends; thank you for always being there for me, especially my beloved Mr. & Mrs. John and Olanike Verissimo, Mrs. Theresa Ajao, Mr. & Mrs. Gbolahan and Bukky Mogaji, Mrs. Faith Ibn-Ibrahim, and Titi Phoebe Bangudu who have supported our seminars financially and with their attendance. You have always been a blessing to my life and your generation.

Special thanks go to Mrs. Sola Goriola for suggesting the title to the book, Dr. Sammy Joseph for his suggestions on the book cover, Reverend Bunmi Omidiran for reading the first manuscript. Pastor Shalom Wales for designing the book cover. A very big thank you to all who read the manuscript and helped with advice, endorsements, prayer, and editing.

I also like to thank Pastor. & Mrs. Rufai for their encouragement and prayers. My appreciation goes to Reverend Victoria Lawrence for her support.

Lastly, I want to express my gratitude to all parents who, over the past years, have allowed me to be a blessing to them and their children. You have been blessings to me as well. This book is a tribute to their honesty and their desire to give the best and their encouragement to their children. Thank you for all your support.

I love you all.

ABOUT THE AUTHOR

Nick Nunayon is an education and information technology consultant, inspirational public speaker, life coach, mentor, trainer, tutor, and pastor based in Dartford, Kent, UK. He is the founder and director of Kingsgen Young Leaders' Centre, a non-profit organisation with the aim of ensuring that children and young adults, especially those from disadvantaged backgrounds, have every opportunity to fulfil their full potential, raise aspirations, broaden their horizons, and become leaders

in their fields, as active, prosperous, and successful citizens of the world around them. Nick is also the proprietor of Kingsgen Academy, a supplementary school based in South East London and Kent supporting children and young adults to achieve academic excellence with students in top grammar schools and private schools in the country, including Eton College,
Christ Hospital, Colfe School, and a host of others.

He is the host of numerous seminars, workshops, and conferences on education, finances, relationships, and leadership.

The author received his Masters' degrees in Accounting and Information Technology from London Metropolitan University, a further Master's Degree in Theology from the University of Wales (now known as the University of Bangor), and a certificate in Teaching and Training, and many other certificates and diplomas in accounting, leadership, information technology and Christian ministries. He is presently studying for PhD in Organizational Leadership.

INTRODUCTION

There is treasure in every child that can be unearthed by their parents, though they may not know how to reveal this in their child as result of inadequate knowledge. This book was written because of a desire and passion to educate parents about the UK Educational System, to inform them about current educational issues affecting their children, to enable them to make informed decisions about their children's education, and bring out the best in their children. It will help to empower them to be actively involved in their children's future and make them to achieve the best academic excellence.

Over the last six years, I have been conducting seminars on the UK Educational System, advising parents on their children's education, representing parents in schools, coaching and mentoring children, and providing support to both parents and children. In the process of working with parents, I discovered that many do not understand the UK Educational System fully and therefore lack a full understanding of how to support their children. Many children have been sent to the wrong schools and/or performed below their abilities because their parents may not have been well informed before important decisions concerning their education were made. I started tutoring in 2008 by preparing my daughter for the Eleven Plus examination, which she passed with flying colours. She was offered places in three grammar schools, one of which was a governor's list admission.

Our supplementary school, Kingsgen Academy, started as a result of demand from parents attending our seminars in 2010. Some of our pupils are in the top grammar schools and private schools in the country, including Eton College, Christ Hospital,

Colfe School, and a host of others.

This book contains everything I have discovered, learnt from other people, taught, and practised as a speaker and tutor. It also contains other parents' experiences, teachers' experiences, and feedback from my tutees, mentees, and their parents over the last six years. The book will help to equip parents to support their children throughout their educational journey. Parents will also learn from other parents' and children's experiences and testimonials.

Enjoy it!

Revised edition

This book has been updated with the recent changes in the UK Educational System. New grades are now in use in primary schools for English, maths and science in secondary schools, while old grades are still in use for other subjects, but this will be phased out gradually. The progress of each student is now taken into consideration when judging schools' performance and publishing their results. Some other updated factors have been added to this current edition.

Your child has a TREASURE in him or her.

CHAPTER 1

Overview of the UK Educational System

One of the things I have discovered from talking to parents about the education of their children is that many do not fully understand the UK Education System. This is one of the topics I speak about in most of my educational seminars and programmes organised for children and adults across the UK. There are five stages of education:

1. Early Years
2. Primary
3. Secondary
4. Further Education (FE)
5. Higher Education (HE)

In the UK, education is compulsory for all children between the ages of 5 and 18. Further education, which covers general or more advanced education, can be taken at further (including tertiary) education colleges and Higher Education Institutions (HEIs), though this is not compulsory. The fifth stage, Higher Education, is study beyond GCSE, A levels, and their equivalent, which, for most full-time students, takes place in universities and other HEIs and colleges. According to the government website, gov.uk, the school leaving age depends on where you live.

England

You can leave school on the last Friday in June if you are 16 by the end of the summer holidays.

You must then do one of the following until you're 18:

- stay in full-time education, for example at a college
- start an apprenticeship or traineeship
- spend 20 hours or more a week working or volunteering, while in part-time education or training

Scotland

If you turn 16 between the 1st of March and 30th of September, you can leave school after the 31st of May of that year.

If you turn 16 between the 1st of October and the end of February, you can leave at the start of the Christmas holidays in that school year.

Wales

You can leave school on the last Friday in June, as long as you are 16 by the end of that school year's summer holidays.

Northern Ireland

If you turn 16 during the school year (between the 1st of September and the 1st of July), you can leave school after the 30th June.

If you turn 16 between the 2nd of July and the 31st of August, you can't leave school until the 30th of June the following year.

The scope of this book is limited to the first three stages of the UK Education System, which are Early Years, Primary, and Secondary education.

Early Years Education

In England, since September 2010, all 3- and 4-year-olds are entitled to 15 hours of free nursery education for 38 weeks of the year; some 2-year-olds are also eligible. Early Years education takes place in a variety of settings, including state nursery schools, nursery classes, and reception classes within primary schools, as well as settings outside the state sector such as voluntary pre-schools, privately-run nurseries, or with child-minders.

In recent years, there has been a major expansion of Early Years education and childcare. The Education Act (2002) extended the National Curriculum for England to include the Foundation Stage, which was first introduced in September 2000 and covered children's education from the age of 3 to the end of the reception year (5 years of age). The Early Years

Foundation Stage (EYFS) came into force in September 2008 and is a single regulatory and quality framework for the provision of learning, development, and care for children in all registered Early Years settings between birth and the academic year in which they turn 5. The EYFS Profile (EYFSP) is the statutory assessment of each child's development and learning achievements at the end of the academic year in which they turn five.[1]

You can start claiming free early education after your child turns 3. The date you can claim will depend on when their birthday is. See Table 1 below for more information.

[1] Education System in the UK

https://www.gov.uk/government/uploads/system/uploads/attachment_data/file/255081/v01_2013ukes.pdf

Table 1

Child's birthday	
1st January to 31st March	beginning of term on or after April 1st
1st April to 31st August	beginning of term on or after September 1st
1st September to 31st December	Beginning of term on or after January 1st

Example

If your child was born on the 15th of February, 2012, they will become eligible for free early education from the start of term following the 1st of April, 2015.[2]

My advice to parents would be to look at their local pre-schools and choose the one they feel most suited to their child. Most pre-schools allow parents and children to visit and observe what goes on in their school. The location of the pre-school should also be considered.

If you are able to secure a nursery school place for your child in a school that has an adjoining primary school, you should be aware that this does not guarantee your child a place in the adjoining primary school. Many parents were unaware of this and found

---

[2] https://www.gov.uk/free-early-education

themselves in an unfortunate situation when the primary school allocation was published.

Primary Schools in the UK

In England, the primary stage covers three age ranges: Nursery (under 4 years of age), Infants (4 to 7 years of age, also known as Key Stage 1, KS1) and Juniors (up to 10 or 11 years, also known as Key Stage 2, KS2). In Scotland and Northern Ireland, there is generally no distinction between infant and junior schools. In Wales, although the types of schools are the same, the Foundation Phase has brought together what was previously known as the Early Years (for 3 to 4 year olds) and Key Stage 1 (for 4 to 7 year olds) of the National Curriculum to create one phase of education for children aged between 3 and 7. Some primary schools have a nursery or children's centre attached to cater for younger children. Most public sector primary schools take both boys and girls in mixed classes.

The main goals of primary education are to ensure that children achieve basic literacy and numeracy skills as well as establishing foundations in science, mathematics, and other subjects. Children in England and Northern Ireland are assessed at the end of Key Stages 1 and 2. In Wales, all children in their final year of Foundation Phase and Key Stage 2 must be assessed with teacher assessments.

The assessment is graded with levels from 1 to 6 (previously 5). To achieve each level, each pupil must meet certain criteria. All levels are awarded either an A, B or C sub-level, so, for example, a Standard Assessment Test (SAT) result may be either 4A, 4B or 4C for the child to be considered as having achieved a level 4.

At the end of Key Stage 2, a child is expected to leave primary school with a level 4 in SATs for maths, English, and science, according to government standards. However, some children finish with a level 5 or 6 in these subjects.

In the last three years, over 80% of our pupils from Kingsgen Academy finished with a level 6 in maths, and more than 70% finished with a level 6 in both maths and English. This provides students with a very good foundation for secondary school as most of the work they do in years 7 and 8 is an extension of what they have done during the Eleven Plus and SATs preparations with us. My son came back home from school and said, "Dad, could you believe some of the questions I practised during my level 6 preparation came out during my year 8 end of year summative assessment?" He was attending one of the top grammar schools in the country. It has been the same story for most of our pupils as we prepare them for both the present and future, which is to pass their Eleven Plus, have a very good foundation for secondary school, and achieve academic excellence. The grading system has changed and you will read more about the new grading system in a later part of this book.

Secondary Schools in the UK

In England, public provision of secondary education may consist of a combination of different types of schools in a pattern that reflects historical circumstances and the policy adopted by the local authority. Secondary schools are generally state funded or independent (known as private schools).

Transferring to a secondary school in the UK can be daunting and stressful if parents do not have an understanding of the education system. Many pupils have missed out on the opportunity to attend the best secondary schools in the country as a result of their parents' lack of knowledge. If you start early enough in planning your child's future, you will find it easier to make informed decisions and prevent as much stress as possible for you and your child when it comes to secondary school education.

Over the past years of tutoring and counselling, I have met many parents who have found themselves in this dilemma. Every local authority has different rules for admissions to secondary schools; the rules may even be different for individual schools within the same local authority. Foundation schools, Voluntary Aided Schools (faith schools), and academies can set their own admissions criteria. There are so many variations in admissions policies, so it is not only important but essential that parents thoroughly research the admissions policies of the schools they choose to apply to form. Now let us look at the types of secondary schools we have in the UK, starting with state-funded schools.

Comprehensive schools

Comprehensive schools largely admit pupils without reference to ability or aptitude, and cater for all children in a particular neighbourhood. However, in some areas, they co-exist with other types of schools; for example, the school may have a grammar school stream, such as with the Erith School in Bexley, Kent; Sydney Russell School in Dagenham, Essex; Crown Woods College in Eltham, Greenwich, South

London; Riverside School in Barking, Essex; and Platanos College in Stockwell, South London.
This type of school is called "bilateral school".

Many parents have condemned comprehensive schools as having poor quality education, even though some comprehensive schools in the country are performing as well as grammar schools. Excellent schools are managed by excellent leaders. The performance of every school depends on the leadership and management of the school. Some parents and commentators blame the performance of comprehensive schools on their intake of lower ability pupils (or those 'left over' from the selective system), but some comprehensives are now producing outstanding results (examples include the London Oratory School, Coloma School in Croydon, London, Plumstead Manor in South East London, Woolwich

Polytechnic in South East London, St. Catherine's Catholic School, the Haberdasher Schools both in South East London, and many others). A comprehensive school could be an academy or free school. The meaning of these terms is explained later in the book.

Grammar schools

Grammar schools are state-funded selective secondary schools in the UK. They are selective because 10-11-year olds have to complete a test called the Eleven Plus before they can be considered for admission into a grammar school. We currently have 164 grammar schools in England. England used to have more than this until many were closed and converted into comprehensive schools in the 60's and 70's.

While there are different admissions criteria for most grammar schools, the first and most common criteria is that pupils pass the Eleven Plus test before they are considered for a place. After this, potential students have to satisfy the school's published over-subscription criteria, such as geographical location, siblings attending the school, and so on. It is very important for parents to check individual grammar schools' over-subscription criteria so they can be well prepared for it. Some parents have won places for their children through appeal if they were turned down as result of not meeting other criteria. The most important thing is passing the Eleven Plus test as parents are given the opportunity to move home before a certain date (known as "cut-off" date) where they can still change their home address to the catchment area in order to be considered for their preferred school if that is part of the admission criteria. For some super selective secondary schools, the only criteria is passing the test, thus disregarding where you live or your distance from the school. They are more interested in educating the brightest and smartest pupils. Such schools include St. Olave's Grammar School in Orpington and Rochester Grammar School in Rochester, Medway.

In 2013, the coalition government provided an opportunity to current grammar schools to expand by increasing their intakes, or to start another school campus in a different location. Some of them have increased the number of intakes while others have begun the plan of starting campuses in another location such as Sevenoaks in Kent. The only condition is that the expansion has to be the same as the sponsored school. For example, if the sponsored school is a single sex school, the new expansion also has to be single sex; otherwise, it will not be approved by the Education Secretary.

The Eleven Plus tests in England have caused controversy for many years. While some parents are calling for the test to be scrapped, others claim that the benefit of sending your child to a grammar school demonstrates the value of such tests. Councils have rejected scrapping the Eleven Plus exam but have decided to change their testing formats and providers. Grammar schools are the alternative to a private/independent education in the UK.

How do we demystify the Eleven Plus test and process? The answer to this question is covered in detail in Chapter 4.

Academies

Academies operating in England are state-funded schools that are not under the control of their local councils. Academies benefit from greater freedoms to help innovate and raise standards. These include freedom from local authority control; the ability to set their own pay and conditions for staff; freedom around the delivery of the curriculum; and the ability to change the lengths of terms and school days.

The Academies Programme was first introduced in March 2000 with the objective of replacing poorly performing schools. Academies were established and driven by external sponsors, to achieve a transformation in education performance. The focus changed in 2010 and the Academies Programme was expanded through legislation in the Academies Act, 2010. This enabled all state-maintained primary, secondary, and special schools to apply to become an academy. The early focus from 2010 was on schools rated 'outstanding' by the Office for Standards in Education, Children's Services and Skills (Ofsted), and the first of these new academies opened in September, 2010. These schools do not have a sponsor but are expected to work with underperforming schools to help raise standards and to support other schools. Most grammar and comprehensive schools with academy status are now working with some primary schools, also known as their feeder schools; they also work in partnership with some comprehensive schools to raise standards and share skills with them.

Free schools

This is one of the Conservative education initiatives and was inspired by the example of Swedish Free and

American Charter Schools. They are set up by parents, teachers, charities, businesses, universities, existing schools, and faith groups. According to the Act in 2010 that established free schools, faith groups can only select 50 per cent of the pupils on the basis of their faith.

These schools are independent of local authority control and enjoy the same privileges and freedom as academies. The first free school (established in 2011) was the London Free School, and it was championed by the journalist, Toby Young.

Free schools, like academies, set their own admission criteria, employ their staff, and set their salary scales. Some free schools (like the London Free School) offer a curriculum centered on traditional and classical academic subjects such as Latin, Divinity and Classical Civilisation, whilst the Greenwich Free School added

Politics, Philosophy and Economics to their curriculum. Some of the Free Schools offer an extended school day until 5.00 or 5.30pm, which can be used for supervised homework and extra curriculum activities such as sports. This differentiates one school from another.

Age, School Year, Government Expected Level

Please be aware that there have been talks very recently to discontinue the use of LEVELS as an indicator of a child's ability; new descriptors have been suggested, especially for KS3 and KS4/GCSE

Please see Appendix 1 for more information.

The government expected levels are average levels set by the government for children of a certain age to achieve, but many children are now achieving above the government levels right from KS1. Most of our pupils at Kingsgen Academy achieve level 4 in Year 4, which is the government's expected level at the end of Year 6, and achieve between Level 5 and Level 6 at the end of Year 6.

The levels are assessed through tests conducted by the teachers and the Standard Assessment Tests known as SATs. SATs are conducted twice throughout the primary school years, at the ends of Key Stage 1 (Year 2) and Key Stage 2 (Year 6).

Children will always achieve above these levels if they are supported by parents either through external tutoring or home tutoring.

In secondary school, children are expected to achieve grade 1-9 by the end of Year 11, and 5 GCSEs at grade 4/5. There are problems with these expected government levels as schools' performances are measured against government targets. Some comprehensive schools are happy to achieve the government's expected level of a good percentage of 5 grades—4/5 which, is former 'C' at GCSE, as it ticks the boxes. However, many schools are pushing their children to achieve over 5 grades—9/8, which is the former 'A*- A', especially the grammar schools. I attended a meeting in a secondary school in South East London and the head teacher confessed that previously they were happy for their students to achieve level "Cs" (5/4) but now they are working towards pushing them to achieve levels A*- C (9-5/4). This is one of the reasons why parents need to monitor their children's school performance, ask teachers questions during parents' evenings, and make sure that their children are working above the teachers' targets.

The GCSE examination is externally administered; therefore, children can exceed their teachers' targets and predicted grades if they work for it. Some comprehensive schools enter their students for GCSEs early in order to achieve the "C", which is now 5/4 grade as this gives them the opportunity to do fewer subjects in their Year 11 examinations, which also helps them to pass the other subjects as well, mostly with "C" grades. The present government stopped this in 2014 as many students would have performed better if they had waited to take the exams in Year 11 instead of in Years 9 and 10. I have heard of a few cases where parents were unhappy with their children's grades as a result of early entry. Some children had to repeat the exams in Year 11 and some had to use the external candidates' route for their children to take the exams again.

In 2014, the government introduced the first entry rule to discourage schools from registering their students for early entry. From 2014, the entry rule ensures that only the result achieved during the first sitting will count towards the school's league or performance table. While some secondary schools are still registering their students for early entries, the percentage is very low now.

Table 2 below provides a summary of school levels by child ages.

Table 2

Key Stage	Age	School Year
Foundation Class	3-4	Nursery
Foundation Class	4-5	Reception Class
KS1	5-6	Year 1
KS1	6-7	Year 2
KS2	7-8	Year 3
KS2	8-9	Year 4
KS2	9-10	Year 5
KS2	10-11	Year 6
KS3	11-14	Year 7-9
KS4	14-16	Year 10-11

Reporting to parents

Annual reports

According to the Government 2017 Assessment and Reporting Arrangements documents as published by the Standards and Testing Agency in October 2016, Head teachers at maintained schools, including maintained special schools, must prepare annual reports for every pupil's parents. Head teachers must make arrangements for parents to discuss the report with their child's teacher, if the parents request it.

The term 'parent' is used here as defined in section 576 of the Education Act, 1996:

- A parent of a pupil
- Any person who is not a parent of a pupil but who has parental responsibility for the pupil

- Any person who has care of a pupil

TA in the context means Teachers' Assessment

What reports must cover:

The report must start from the day after the last report was given. It must be available to parents before the end of the summer term.

The report must cover the pupil's:

- Achievements
- General progress
- Attendance record

At KS1, it must also include:

- Outcomes of the statutory national curriculum Teacher Assessment (TA) in English reading, English writing, mathematics and science

- A statement that TA outcomes take into account the results of statutory national curriculum tests in English reading and mathematics

- Where appropriate, a statement explaining why any national curriculum test has not been taken

At the end of the academic year, KS1 English reading, English writing, and mathematics TAs are the outcomes used for accountability. For pupils who have completed the KS1 programme of study, teachers will use interim TA frameworks when making their judgements. The frameworks contain three standards that are reported as follows:

- Working towards the expected standard

- Working at the expected standard

- Working at greater depth within the expected standard

For KS1 English reading, English writing, and mathematics, pupils who are not yet 'working towards the expected standard' should be assessed using the interim pre-key stage standards.[3]

At KS2, it must also include:

- The results of any national curriculum tests taken, including the pupil's scaled score and whether or not they met the 'expected standard'
- The outcomes of statutory national curriculum TA in English reading, English writing, mathematics, and science
- Where appropriate, a statement explaining why any national curriculum test has not been taken

---

[3] https://www.gov.uk/government/publications/2017-key-stage-1-assessment-and-reporting-arrangements-ara

If a parent requests access to their child's national curriculum test results, this must be made available to them.

For maintained schools, it is a requirement that reports include pupils' general progress in statutory subjects. This includes subjects within the KS1 national curriculum as well as religious education, unless a child has been withdrawn from this subject by their parents (under Section 71 of the School Standards and Framework Act 1998)

The national curriculum tests at the end of KS2 (often referred to as SATs) are administered in mathematics, English reading, and English grammar, punctuation, and spelling.

KS2 are now graded after the end of year assessment with the new graded system:

Each pupil registered for the tests will receive:

- A raw score (the number of marks awarded)
- A scaled score
- Confirmation of whether or not they met the 'expected standard'

Calculating raw scores

The raw scores for each test are calculated by adding the scores from each paper for a subject, as detailed below in Table 3.[4]

[4] https://www.gov.uk/government/publications/2017-key-stage-2-assessment-and-reporting-arrangements-ara

Test	Number of marks available in the paper	Total number of test marks available – highest raw score
English	50 marks	50 marks
English grammar, punctuation and spelling Paper 1: questions	50 marks	70 marks
English grammar, punctuation and spelling Paper 2: spelling	20 marks	
Mathematics Paper 1: arithmetic	40 marks	110 marks
Mathematics Paper 2: reasoning	35 marks	
Mathematics Paper 3: reasoning	35 marks	

Scaled scores are used to report national curriculum test outcomes. A scaled score of 100 represents the 'expected standard' for the KS2 tests.

What is a scaled score?

A pupil's scaled score is based on their raw score. The raw score is the total number of marks a pupil scores in a test, based on the number of questions they answered correctly.

We develop tests each year to the same specification, but because the questions must be different, the difficulty of tests may vary slightly each year. This means we need to convert the raw scores pupils get in the tests into a scaled score, to ensure we can make accurate comparisons of pupil performance over time. Every scaled score will represent the same level of attainment for a pupil each year, so a pupil who scores

103, for example, in 2016 will have demonstrated the same attainment as a pupil who scores 103 in 2017.

A scaled score of 100 will always represent the expected standard on the test. Pupils scoring 100 or more will have met the expected standard.

Panels of teachers set the raw score required to meet the expected standard on each test.

The range of scaled scores available for each KS2 test is the same and will stay the same in future years:

- 80 is the lowest scaled score that can be awarded
- 120 is the highest scaled score

A pupil awarded a scaled score of 100 or more has met the expected standard in each test.

A pupil awarded a scaled score of 99 or less has not met the expected standard in the test.

As tests and TAs are different forms of assessment, they do not report using the same scale. As a result, there are no scaled score equivalents to the TA concepts of 'working towards the expected standard' or 'working at greater depth within the expected standard'.

If a pupil has not scored enough marks on the test to demonstrate that they have sufficient understanding of the KS2 curriculum for the subject, they will not receive a scaled score. The scaled score field for the pupil in the return of results section will be left blank. The outcome of the test for the pupil will be 'NS', meaning the expected standard was not achieved.

CHAPTER 2

The Primary School Admission Process

Some primary schools in the UK have nursery schools where children can start at the age of 3 for about 3 hours a day and some children are moved to the reception year at the age of 4 or 5 years, depending on their date of birth. Over the years, things have changed and the fact that a child is attending a nursery school affiliated with a primary school does not guarantee an automatic place in the reception year of that primary school. It is very important that you apply to the council even if your child is attending a nursery school owned by a primary school. The following steps should be taken when applying to reception class in a primary school:

- Complete the online council form between the 30th of September and the 15th of January.

- Select six schools according to your preference (always remember the criteria of your preferences).
- The council will send you an offer on or around the 16th of April before the September of the starting year.
- If you are happy with the offer, send your acceptance back to the council.
- If you are not happy with the offer, or you were not given your preferred school, you can reject the offer and appeal to the council.
- I do advise parents to accept the offer instead of rejecting it and then appeal to the council. This is because if a parent rejects the offer and then loses the appeal, it will be their responsibility to find a school for their child unless they accept

any other schools the council offers them after the allocation.

- All appeals must be submitted to the council on or before the 16th of May that same year. Please check these dates with your council as they change every year.

If you need any help completing the council form or appealing, contact our consultancy services through www.kingsgen.co.uk or www.kingsgenacademy.co.uk and we will be happy to assist you.

CHAPTER 3

The Secondary School Admissions Process

The route to secondary school depends on the type you want your child to attend: comprehensive, grammar, or independent (private).

Comprehensive schools

There is no test or exam for selection, although some schools test on NVR (Non-Verbal Reasoning) and use it for banding allocation. Most comprehensive school selection is based on their admission criteria so parents are advised to check these before they apply.

Comprehensive schools include:

1. Free schools
2. Academies
3. Any other non-selective school

Grammar schools

For a grammar school, the admissions process starts with the Eleven Plus test, for which parents have to register their children. Most primary schools do not support preparation for the tests; however, some schools indirectly support the children by establishing an "After School Eleven Plus Club." These are common in some Kent schools. The preparation for the Eleven Plus test is solely the parents' responsibility. Detailed information on grammar schools and how to get your child into a one is available in Chapter 4.

Private secondary schools

For private secondary schools (also known as independent secondary schools in the UK), the admissions policy and entrance tests are outside government regulations as these are fee-paying schools. A private school can be a day school, a boarding school, or a combination of both. A child can apply to both a private school and a government-maintained school at the same time.

Detailed information on private schools and how to get your child into one is available in Chapter 11.

CHAPTER 4

The Eleven Plus and Common Entrance Examinations

The Eleven Plus test is part of the admissions process into selective secondary schools in the UK. It is used by grammar schools and private schools to assess students who transfer to senior school at the ages of 11 and 13. Private schools refer to this test as the Common Entrance Test. In the UK, there are currently about 164 grammar schools, and many private schools.

The Eleven Plus tests are completed in the September (for grammar schools) or the January (for most private schools) of the year the pupils start Year 6. The tests for grammar schools may be administered by the local council, consortiums, or individual schools. Read more on the private schools admission process in Chapter 11.

Providers of the Eleven Plus test in the UK

There are different providers of the Eleven Plus test; the choice will depend on the council and the school administering the test. The providers of the test for State Grammar schools are GL Assessment, CEM University Durham, and the Consortium of Selective Schools in Essex (CSSE). Some Grammar schools administer their own Eleven Plus tests. These include: St Olave's Grammar School Orpington, Kent; Newstead Wood Grammar School Orpington, Kent; Chelmsford County High School for Girls. Some grammar schools in Kent County are now administering the Eleven Plus in addition to the Kent county test. The test is used to judge pupils' suitability for a grammar school place if they are not judged suitable with the Kent exam. Such schools are

Mayfield Grammar School, Gravesend, Dover Grammar School for boys, and few others.

How and when to start preparing for the Eleven Plus

Many parents leave the preparation for the Eleven Plus test until their child is in Year 5, but this has worked to the disadvantage of many pupils. Some smart and bright pupils with short preparation times do pass the test, but I have seen many fail the test as well due to late preparation.

There is no particular school year or age to start preparing your child for the Eleven Plus or the Common Entrance Test. Start working with them and make sure they are exceeding the National Curriculum targets as early as possible.

A child's academic excellence is more than just passing the Eleven Plus test. I have prepared a few pupils in the late starter group for between six and ten hours before the test and they passed the Eleven Plus with very high scores. You can read about them in the testimonials section. Children with strong academic excellence have gone on to be in the top set in their respective grammar schools, while students without a strong foundation struggle until they start getting support from parents or tutors. From the onset, parents should aim for their children's academic excellence rather than simply passing the Eleven Plus test as this helps pupils gain a very strong foundation and a better attitude to learning compared to pupils who were solely prepared to pass the Eleven Plus test.

Eleven Plus preparation starts when a child starts school not when a child is about to transfer to secondary school.

A few years ago while travelling by train to Disneyland in Paris, our 3-year-old son saw an electricity pole with two branches and he started pointing out of the window and telling us "that is letter Y". I did not understand what he was saying initially until we all looked at the pole and saw that its shape was "letter Y". What a brilliant way to recognise the alphabet! Most of the time, we use things around us to teach our children, which is creative teaching in one sense. This is the same boy who went on to pass the Eleven Plus a year early for a super selective top grammar school known as St. Olave's Grammar School. He also passed the National SATs with level 6, passed the GCSE maths higher linear exam with an "A" when he was eleven, and passed the Eton entrance examination and is now a bona fide student of Eton College. Our daughter has won awards in secondary school, went to prestigious Dartford Grammar School for her sixth form and now in a Russell Group University. We give glory to God for all these achievements and accolades, but there is price to be paid for every achievement.

Early support for your child will build a very strong academic foundation in them, and I strongly encourage parents to start supporting their children as early as possible instead of waiting until they are in Year 4 or 5.

Some children attending private schools who will be sitting the same test as your child are two years above the state school curriculum. Even if your child is not going to grammar school or private school, the name of the game is: "Start early with your child."

I have encountered parents who attended our seminars, practising everything they learned with their children, and you can see smiles on their faces when they meet me and tell me of their children's achievements. Some of these parents were mentored or advised by me and I always rejoice and give praise to the glory to God whenever they share these testimonies of their children's achievements with me. I have cards from my pupils that I find difficult to throw away. I have had a Sainsbury's gift card for four years. I have a text message from one of my pupils I could not delete. Recently, one of my pupils called me and announced her Level 6 SATs result to me. I am always excited and feel fulfilled when children call me to announce their achievements and awards. I am very happy seeing other children achieving what our children are achieving as well. I have added some of their testimonials at the end of this book.

In 2013, most of the pupils who attended our tuition centre were below average, and it was very unfortunate that this was the year most councils changed their test format and provider. That year, we had our lowest pass rate of 80%, but the Eleven Plus test results were generally very bad in the whole of Kent and Bexley. Before the changes to the format of the test, it was easier for us to prepare average pupils to pass if they worked hard on the 21 types of Verbal Reasoning (VR) and 6 types of Non-Verbal Reasoning (NVR) tests, performed above average in mathematics, and worked according to my instructions.

Apart from maths and English comprehension and creative writing, councils also test the reasoning ability of students using VR and NVR tests. A very good foundation in maths and English will help both VR and NVR as VR consists of vocabulary, word building, patterns, sequences, spellings, synonyms, antonyms, logic, anagrams, clauses, and proof reading, and NVR consists of shapes, codes, patterns and logical deduction, sequences, and recognising 3D shapes. Children who are engaged in games, puzzles, and word searches do better in the reasoning tests than other pupils. Reading books and magazines will also help pupils to learn new words and build their vocabulary, which will improve their knowledge of synonyms and antonyms. Pupils can learn maths from their daily activities, such as helping with shopping in supermarkets. They should be given the opportunity to compare prices, add prices together, etc. My two children learned some of these from an early age, and they have always been in the top mathematics and English sets in their respective grammar schools. Help children to see maths as something to play with like a game rather than a scary monster. Ensure that they master the four operational mathematical signs (+, -, x, ÷), which are the basic skills in maths.

You do not necessarily need a tutor to work with your children, until it gets to the point where you cannot cope with their school work as result of your inadequacies, time, or patience.

As children take the Eleven Plus tests in Year 6 (September), Year 5 should be used for filling the gaps and practising familiarisation with papers from different authors and test providers.

Visit the grammar schools with your child early, maybe when they are in Year 3. I know parents who have done this to prepare the minds of their children.

Connect your children with other children who are already in grammar schools so they can start discussing it early; this will also paint a picture in your child's mind. Find ways to inspire your children!

Eleven Plus examination preparatory materials

There are many resources available for Eleven Plus test preparation, but parents should be careful and speak with their children's tutors or seek advice from Eleven Plus forums before buying them. Some of these are foundation materials while others have varying levels of difficulty, some of which are even more difficult than the actual Eleven Plus test questions. Therefore, children who practice with these difficult materials are more likely to pass the Eleven Plus tests. The most popular among these materials are the Bond series, which have become a household name; however, there are many other books that are suitable and better for the test. Good maths and English books are the most important foundation books for children of any age, and the Eleven Plus materials can be added to them when the children are in Year 5. Children should be encouraged to start reading good fiction and non-fiction books from an early age. You can borrow many of these books from your local library.

It is very important that children practice the familiarisation papers for the Eleven Plus test relevant to the grammar school they are applying to. The familiarisation papers given by the councils or exam boards will help with the format of the test, but here is a warning to all parents:

Do not rely on the strength of the papers. Children have relied on the content and were disappointed during the test as the practice tests were easier than the actual tests.

Start Eleven Plus practice with easy material and end with the harder ones; most of the time when children start with the harder ones, it demoralises them as a result of achieving a low score.

As mentioned earlier, you do not necessarily need a tutor to work with your children. I do encourage parents to tutor their children, but they have to be honest with themselves as to whether they are achieving their targets with their children. It is not enough to have the books; having the techniques and patience needed for teaching children is also very important, and some parents do not have these. On a few occasions, I have tutored children whose parents are teachers. I have also tutored children whose parents are tutoring other people's children but find they cannot tutor their own. I do encourage parents to start teaching their children when they are toddlers and infants. I also encourage parents to build a bond with their children. This can happen through creating time to teach and relate with the children.

Test Day

It is very important for parents to check the test information sent to them before the test day. If possible, they should locate the test centre before the test day. Some parents have made the mistake of taking their children to the wrong centres, especially in areas where boys and girls are separated into single sex schools.

I suggest (based on my own experience) that two adults should travel with the child to the test centre on the day of the test as there may be traffic problems on that day. If there are traffic problems, one adult can walk to the test centre with the child whilst the other one sorts out the car and parking.

The night before the test, children should go to bed early enough to have a good night's sleep and to relax their minds in preparation for the next day.

Parents should discuss things that have nothing to do with the test with their children to relax their minds and take the anxiety and tension away from them. All revision should have been done before that evening.

Children should wake up early to get ready for the test if it is taking place away from their primary school.

Parents should endeavour to arrive early in order to avoid rushing, which increases their child's tension and stress.

Check that your child has more than one pencil properly sharpened, a rubber, and a sharpener before leaving home. Every second spent sharpening a pencil will reduce time spent on their question paper.

Encourage them to follow all the instructions given to them during the test.

What happens after the test?
Councils and schools will publish the test results in the second week of October. If your child is successful, the next step is to decide which grammar school you want him or her to attend (tips on how to do this are discussed in the next chapter). If your child does not make the cut-off mark, you can appeal after choosing your state secondary school, although

in Kent and some councils, the head teacher of your child's primary school has the option to request a 'Head Teacher Assessment' if they think your child has the ability to do well at the grammar school before the result is available to parents.

What is a Head Teacher Assessment?

A 'Head Teacher Assessment' is part of the Eleven Plus process in some councils administering Eleven Plus tests. It is also referred to as a 'Head Teacher Appeal' or 'Head Teacher Review'.

Primary school head teachers receive the results of the Eleven Plus test at the beginning of October. After studying the results, some councils give the head teachers the opportunity to request a 'Head Teacher Assessment' for children who do not reach the required pass standard. This is quite different from the appeal that normally takes place after school offers have been made to parents as it is carried out confidentially without the knowledge of the child or their parents. For the Kent Eleven Plus tests, the child's head teacher will submit the child's school work and reports to the Head Teacher's Panel, who review all the work submitted, mark the extended writing task, and make a final decision. If the child is considered suitable for grammar school, the decision is regarded as a pass on an equal footing with those who gained automatic selection through test results. In Medway Council, parents can request that their children's scores be reviewed after getting their result; this is not the same thing as an appeal.

Some parents who live outside Kent have complained to me that their children's head teachers were not aware of the 'Head Teacher Assessment'. I contacted the Kent County School Admissions board who confirmed to me that all the information is sent with the Eleven Plus test results to all primary school head teachers. It is up to the head teachers to read all the information and take the necessary steps. The honest truth is that not many head teachers support the grammar school system and do nothing to help their pupils as a result. It is important for parents to let the head teachers know that their children are taking the Eleven Plus test and that the head teacher should appeal on behalf of the child if the child does not meet the required mark but is working at above level 4A in both maths and English. This should be put in writing after discussing it with the head teacher as a backup. It is important to note that appealing or review is at the discretion of the head teachers and will depend on several factors.

However, if your child is attending a primary school that supports the Eleven Plus tests and encourages children to attend grammar schools, the head teacher knows what to do if your child's academic performance and behaviour are good.

CHAPTER 5

How to Choose the Right School?

When choosing a school for your child, consider the following points and make your own judgements on them:

1. Academic performance of the school as shown in the league tables

This is very popular among many parents, although some parents do not really understand the academic performance of schools based on the information provided in the league tables.

For primary schools, ask and search for the Level 4, 5 and 6 SATs percentages in maths and English (reading and writing). Check for the number of children who sat the exams and the pass rate in comparison to other schools.

For secondary schools, ask about their percentage of A*- C or 9-4, which is equivalent to the old GCSE grades focusing on English, maths, and science.

For example:

- How many gained an A* or 9 in English, maths, and science?
- How many gained an A or 8 in English, maths, and science?
- How many gained a B or 7/6 in English, maths, and science?
- How many gained a C or 5/4 in English, maths, and science?

The breakdown or analysis of these grades will help parents uncover how academically good the school is as some do rely on C or 5/4 grades to satisfy government performance requirements. Do not rely on the A*- C or 9-4 percentage. The present grading system for secondary schools is now taking the progress schools made with a student into consideration, which is the concept of 'value added'. The value-added approach provides fair comparisons between the progress made by students in a single school or college with a large sample of the others in the various project. To make these comparisons, the students need to be measured against a common baseline assessment before they take their KS3 SATs, GCSEs, or A2 examinations.

2. The Ofsted Report

Ofsted is the body that inspects most schools and prepares a report based on their judgements of the following:

- Effectiveness of leadership and management.
- Quality of teaching, learning, and assessment.
- Personal development, behaviour, and welfare.
- Outcomes for children and learners.

The Ofsted Report groups schools into one of five categories:

Grade 1 - Outstanding

An outstanding school is highly effective in delivering outcomes that provide exceptional help for all its pupils' needs. This ensures that pupils are very well equipped for the next stage of their education, training, or employment.

Grade 2 - Good

A good school is effective in delivering outcomes that well provide for all its pupils' needs. Pupils are well prepared for the next stage of their education, training, or employment.

Grade 3 - Requires improvement

A school that requires improvement is not yet a good school, but is also not inadequate. This school will receive a full inspection within 24 months from the date of the last inspection.

Grade 4 - Inadequate

A school that has serious weaknesses is inadequate overall and requires significant improvement, but leadership and management are judged to be Grade 3 or better. This school will receive regular monitoring by Ofsted inspectors.

Special Measures

A school that requires special measures is one that is failing to give its pupils an acceptable standard of education, and the school's leaders, managers, or governors have not demonstrated they have the capacity to secure the necessary improvements in the school. This school will receive regular monitoring by Ofsted inspectors.

It is important not to rely solely on the Ofsted report because schools prepare for this inspection. I have heard of situations where head teachers send home students the school believes will 'spoil' the inspection. Sometimes it is difficult for Ofsted to see the true picture of the school, and some Ofsted inspectors work privately for, or have links with, some schools. There were stories in the media of schools in Birmingham and Bradford that were not following the normal curriculum, and were teaching the children intolerance towards other religions. Surprisingly, these schools had been inspected before and none of these issues were discovered, reported, or flagged. Check more than one Ofsted report as these will show you if the school has made any improvements from the previous report. A true Ofsted report normally shows the strengths and weaknesses of each school.

3. Speak to schools directly for information

For primary schools, ask about the Eleven Plus and the SATs pass rates for about the past five years and the students' final destination after they leave the school. Some schools may tell you that the government does not permit them to support or interfere with the Eleven Plus (which is true for Kent County and Bexley councils, for example), but some schools indirectly support and prepare their pupils for the Eleven Plus test.

For secondary schools, ask for the list of their school leavers' destinations. The percentage of their students who gain admission into top universities will determine how good the school is in 'value added scores', preparations for further and higher education, and encouraging the students to aim high.

Check the courses they are reading at these top universities as well. Some secondary schools are known for sending a high percentage of students to Oxbridge and Russell group universities to read competitive courses such as medicine, medical science, law, accounting, engineering, and so on. The school plays a role in preparing the students for admission into these competitive courses or provides some support to the students.

4. What support is available to students with lower abilities?

We are now witnessing many financial cuts from the public sector, which includes schools. As a result of this, schools do not have as many teaching assistants as they used to. Although some schools do receive a premium grant from the government for children with lower abilities, not all schools use the money for this purpose.

5. What support is available for children with Additional Educational Needs (AEN)?

Just because a school has good SATs or GCSE results and has received an 'Outstanding' from Ofsted does not mean it is suitable for your child. Ensure that the school has provisions for your child's additional need(s). Ask them if they have such children in their school at the moment. Ask them to show you one of the classes where the child is. Recently, I worked with a child with Asperger's syndrome. He had to choose between three grammar schools (including one of the best in the country), but when his parents visited the three schools and compared their facilities and resources, they decided to go for the third one which, although was not an 'Outstanding' school as compared to the other two, had the facilities to provide for their child's additional needs.

6. What is the provision for more able, high ability, or gifted and talented students?

Educational research has proved that many schools are neglecting children with high ability. Neil O'Brien, director of Policy Exchange, an independent think tank working for better public services, a stronger society, and a more dynamic economy, in his article, "Beyond the grammar schools debate: how can we help bright kids from poorer backgrounds?" commented about schools' provision for high-ability children:

"I think there are lots more pupils capable of high performance than we currently recognise. Indeed, evidence from HMI and Ofsted finds that a lack of intellectual challenge is a consistent feature in lessons in many schools. Some 46% of students found their school work too easy and 42% found their schooling boring."[5]

Polly Curtis, the Guardian's deputy national editor, in her article, "Schools are failing gifted pupils" concurred with the view of Neil O'Brien when she stated that "Thousands of the country's brightest pupils are missing out on tailored teaching because their schools are failing to take part in a programme catering for gifted children."[6]

---

[5] Beyond the grammar schools debate: how can we help bright kids from poorer backgrounds?
http://blogs.telegraph.co.uk/news/neilobrien1/100082619/beyond-the-grammarschools-debate-how-can-we-help-bright-kids-from-poorer-backgrounds/

[6] Polly Curtis Schools are failing gifted pupils,
http://www.theguardian.com/education/2008/sep/19/schools

7. Visit the school during normal school hours

Visit the classroom to observe teachings and observe top, middle, and bottom sets in maths, English, and science. Checking how their activities are differentiated will give ideas on how high ability students are pushed and how the weakest cohort are supported. Ask the students how often homework is given and what happens to those who fail to do it. Take note of their behaviour, dress, and how many children are in the classroom. After the lessons, you can ask the teachers some questions, such as whether their children attend the school or not. Visit during sports day, choir and drama performances and you will discover the true colour or picture of the school.

8. Talk to parents, especially those with children in the school

Not many parents whose children attend the school will give you an honest view of the school, but some may. You can also read parent reviews on the Ofsted website. The website allows parents to rate their children's school and the website address is https://parentsview.ofsted.gov.uk

CHAPTER 6

Common Application Form (CAF)

After you have decided on the secondary school you want your child to attend, you will need to complete the Common Application Form (CAF) online (preferred by most councils) or obtain a paper copy of the form from the primary school (if available). CAFs are processed by the council where you pay your council tax and not the council responsible for your proposed secondary school or your child's current primary school if they attend primary school outside your local council's area. Parents can select five or six schools in order of preference after checking the schools published admission criteria. Your child will be offered the next school on your list if the top school does not offer him or her a place.

Elevenplusexam.co.uk, which provides resources and information on the Eleven Plus to parents, highlighted the following crucial points to remember when completing the CAF:

1. You should always put the schools in your real order of preference.

2. All your preferences must be firmly rooted in reality. If you are desperate for your child to attend a grammar school 20 miles away but the school has never allocated a place to a child living further than 6 miles away, there is no point in listing it on your CAF. However, if you live 8 or 9 miles away from that school, it may be worth taking a gamble, as there may be fewer children applying that year.

3. The further down your CAF preferences you need to go, the more realistic you need to be about the

chances of getting a place. Your last preference should always be a school that will be acceptable to you and your child and one at which your child is certain to get a place – the ultimate fall back if all else fails.

4. If you do not obtain a place at any of your listed preferences, your local authority will allocate you a place at one of their schools that is not yet full. The rules for doing this vary between local authorities and are usually published on their admissions website. Statistics from previous years may suggest which schools are likely to be undersubscribed, but watch out for changes in conditions. If you are absolutely certain which school you would be allocated in this way, you might be able to omit it from your preferences to make room for another school. We would strongly advise you to check

carefully with your Local Admissions Department or with the School Choice Advisers before doing this.

You must submit your completed CAF on or before the published closing date, which, for London councils, is usually the last working day in October. Check with your council for information on closing dates for applications.

Schools normally hold "transfer to secondary school" meetings in March or April. During these meetings, parents are given all the necessary information, including information on how to apply for admission.

Admission offers are sent to parents on the first working day in March. Parents who applied online will receive their allocation from 4pm on that day, while other parents have to wait for the postman on the next day.

Parents whose children are denied places in their school of preference are given the right to appeal to an independent appeal panel. There are two kinds of appeal:

- Selection Appeal
- Transfer Appeal

The Selection Appeal Panel considers appeals for children applying to grammar schools that did not score above the cut-off marks for the Eleven Plus test.

The Transfer Appeal Panel considers appeals from parents whose children were not allocated their preferred schools.

During the appeal process, parents will be given the opportunity to present their reasons of appeal and evidence to support their appeal, and the school will also present the reasons why a place was not offered to the pupil. The panel will listen to both sides and make their decision. The decision of the independent panel has to be honoured by the school; therefore, they will have to create a place for that pupil if this is the decision made.

Parents can state different reasons for their appeal, and parents with appropriate reasons normally win the appeal.

Parents whose children are not offered places as result of over-subscription or being outside the catchment areas but meet the other criteria are given the opportunity to put their children's names on the registered waiting list of the school in case other pupils decline their offer. Some schools maintain the waiting list for two years while some keep it for longer. I advise parents to continue checking with the school, especially after the first offer, as some parents who want their children to attend a private school will decline the offer. It is a well-known fact that places do remain after the first offer in most schools, and more spaces are available after the schools resume in September. You need to continue calling the school after the second week in September, by which point they will know if there are any available spaces.

Twelve Plus and Thirteen Plus

Another opportunity available to students who failed to make the Eleven Plus entrance into grammar school is the Twelve Plus and Thirteen Plus. Twelve

Plus is for students to join grammar school in Year 8 while Thirteen Plus is to join grammar school in Year 9.

The test is administered by individual grammar schools. Students are tested mostly on English, maths, science, and CAT (CAT involves reasoning papers like NVR and VR). The tests normally take place during the summer term preceding the September entry year. I suggest that you should follow this process:

1. Parents need to first contact their council for an in-year admissions form

2. Parents should fill the form with the grammar school of the choice. You can select the number of grammar schools according to the form's permits

3. The council will send your details to the council where the grammar schools are if it is outside your borough

4. If the grammar schools are within your borough, the council will contact them directly

5. The school will contact you with the date of test

You might have to write a test for each school in some councils while at another councils, you can write one test that will cover all the grammar schools of your choice.

6. If your child is successful, the school will contact you with the result and offer of a place if there is one, or put you on their waiting list

In conclusion, passing Twelve Plus and Thirteen Plus are not guaranteed means of entering into grammar school as result of availability of space. I will always advise parents to do their best to support their children passing the Eleven Plus and also meet the necessary criteria of grammar school admissions.

EDUCATION IS THE BEST INVESTMENT

THAT YIELDS THE BEST INTEREST,

DIVIDENDS, AND PROFIT

CHAPTER 7

How Do I Support My Child?

Whether a child is attending a state-funded school or a private school, parents play a major role in the academic achievement of their children. Most children who excel in school are well supported by their parents. As a parent, I have discovered that the level or degree of a parent's relationship with their children will, to an extent, determine the degree of their success in life. As I normally tell parents, a child's achievement is influenced greatly by three factors: parental support, the child's desire to learn and succeed, and the input of the teacher or private tutor.

If these three parties can work together, the child will always perform excellently in school and finish well. As a parent and tutor, I believe I am in a better position to say that I have seen many children doing excellently in both state schools and private schools. Our children are excelling in very good schools because we (my wife and I) supported them from a young age. The right support can greatly improve a child's academic performance. It can enable a lower ability child to become an "able child", and an able child to become 'more able', and so on. Parents often compare private schools with state-funded schools and conclude that private school education is the better option. This is not necessarily the case. Some years ago, I read an article written by a journalist who attended a private school and had children in a private school. In his opinion, the secret of most private schools' achievements is parental support. He concluded that if parents can come together and support state-funded schools, there will be a huge improvement in the schools' and the children's academic achievements. In most of the seminars hosted by the Kingsgen Academy, parents frequently ask how they can support their children given the constraints of work, house chores, and other responsibilities such as studying, church attendance, and so on. The key is to do as much as you can with your child and employ a personal tutor if you are unable to help your child any longer.

One of the problems I have noticed over the years is that many parents support their children during the Eleven Plus preparation but withdraw the support when the children start secondary school, especially if they start a grammar school. This has affected many students as they cannot cope with the demands of the grammar school once they are there. As some of them are average students who were 'microwaved' to pass the Eleven Plus tests, they go downhill and end up not having the self-motivation to meet the demands of the grammar school. Many such students leave the grammar school after their GCSEs and end up in a comprehensive school or a college for their sixth form.

It is very important that parents continue supporting their children after the Eleven Plus exams to ensure they maintain their academic excellence. Children excel with any support given to them, either formal or informal.

Support from private tutors is formal support, while support from parents or friends is informal. Formal or informal additional support is very important for most children to be successful in the competitive world in which we live today. Teachers complain about their workload on a daily basis; each class in a state-funded school contains about 30 students, so it is difficult for children to receive adequate support during lessons. Some teachers are kind enough to assist children who approach them after class, but this is not enough most of the time. Private tutoring is not limited to children in state-funded schools; children attending independent or private schools are also supported with private tutoring. This has been published in the newspapers several times and you can check this on the internet.

1. Be a role model for learning

Parents are their children's first teachers — exploring nature, reading together, cooking together, and learning how to count. When a young child begins formal school, the parents' job is to show him/her how school can extend the learning that began at home and how exciting and meaningful this learning can be. Through guidance and reminders, parents help their children organise their time and support their desire to learn new things in and out of school. Recently, a parent told me how she still remembers how her father made maths simple and easy to understand for her when she was in Year 5 and 6, but she cannot remember anything her private tutor taught her, nor the name of her private tutor or even the tuition centre she attended! Her late father left an imprint on her and instilled in her the value of education. She holds a degree in accounting and is a qualified accountant. If her father had not stepped in, I do not know what her mathematical ability would have been now.

2. Set aside time to read together

Children enjoy having their parents read to them. You need to set aside time to read to your children, especially in the evenings as most children enjoy parents reading to them at bed time. You need to read aloud regularly to your children and when they are able to read, allow them to read to you. If your children are reluctant readers, reading aloud will expose them to the structure and vocabulary of good literature and get them interested in reading more. Reading together with your children will help them gain an interest in reading and develop a reading habit. Do not just ask them to read; discuss what they have read and ask questions that will prompt and develop their thinking and comprehension ability.

3. Study your children to know how they learn

Watch your child to know how they study; for example, whether they are visual learners, auditory learners, or kinaesthetic learners. Visual learners enjoy learning with pictures, watching videos, reading from books or charts, or having somebody explain things to them. Auditory learners learn best by listening to people, tapes, or CDs. Kinaesthetic learners like being involved; they learn through touching and experiencing what they are being taught. They learn by doing and trying things out. It is possible for siblings to have different learning styles, and most children use a combination of styles to study and learn. By paying attention to how your child learns, you may be able to gain their interest and explain difficult concepts in the best possible way to aid their understanding.

4. Go over what your child learns at school

It is very important that you go over what your child learns at school on a daily basis. This will help you to assess whether your child understands what is being taught in school or not. It will also highlight areas they may need extra help with, or areas where they could be further challenged.

Also, go over homework with your child, and ensure that it is done promptly and correctly. Even if you do not know anything about that subject, make sure you still check as students may deceive their parents if they know they will not check their work. Not doing homework puts them into collision with their teachers if they are in a good school. One of my older friends told us a story about his mother when he was in secondary school. His illiterate mother would always ask him to bring his book to show her and any time he did not get everything right, his mother would question it and give him a knock because she believed that if someone else in the class got it right, why not her son! She recognised the 'tick' for right answers and the "x" for wrong answers. You can also read the story of renowned surgeon, Dr. Ben Carson, whose illiterate mother helped him to become a high achiever from his book "Gifted Hands" or watch his videos on

YouTube. You can help your child become an achiever.

5. Relate what your child learns to everyday life

Make learning a part of your child's everyday experience, especially when it comes from your child's natural questions. When you cook together, practise measuring and weighing ingredients. When you are out and about, read the numbers on number plates. Relate everyday things to maths and English.

You can do some mental maths and spelling in the kitchen. You can use whatever you are cooking to teach children how to write a recipe as it is part of the KS2 curriculum. My wife taught our children a lot of things in the kitchen, especially reading together, spellings, and multiplication tables. In fact, we used to have a multiplication table pasted on the wall in our kitchen when our children were young.

6. Connect their school work or learning to the world

Encourage your children to read newspapers and listen to the news. Find out what they know about recent happenings and current affairs. Older children can relate economic and business news easily to what they are learning at school. This will give them an edge over other students as they will have examples to illustrate or support their answers in tests and exams. News of activities around the world, such as hurricanes, earthquakes, and global warming can help with geography and science lessons. Some of the things they learn in GCSE physics can be seen around them in their homes and the environment; for example, an understanding of the heating system in your property and how to conserve energy. Medical apparatus and equipment in hospitals are part of present day science topics.

7. Arrange visits to educational venues such as libraries, museums, and zoos

Visits to educational venues such museums, aquariums, zoos, and nature reserves contribute to enhancing and consolidating children's learning. These activities greatly add to a well-rounded education for children. It also gives them the opportunity to ask their teachers more questions in the classroom, and increases their thirst for knowledge.

Children can develop a positive and better learning attitude and reading habits if they are introduced to the library very early in life. Readers are leaders, and good writers are good readers as well.

8. Help your child take charge of their learning

Children should be kept in charge of their learning by setting their own goals, choosing the goal to work on, on a daily basis, how to achieve their goals, and so on. Parents should only guide on how to have vision, set goals, prioritising and time management, but allow their children to take charge by stepping aside. Children who take charge of their learning become independent learners and high achievers.

9. Control television and game time

Television programmes and computer games can be educational, but also destructive. Research suggests that watching too much television does not give children the opportunity to develop and enhance their own interests. Restrict television and game time, for example, to just an hour a day or at the weekends, and ensure that school work, house chores, and any other important activities are done before this time.

10. Create the right environment for learning

Children need a quiet, organised space for studying. This can be a desk or even a spot at the dining room table. Ensure that they have all the things they need for their learning, including stationery, paper, calculators, and a dictionary.

Make an effort to attend parents' evenings

Schools organise parents' evenings at least once a year for each year group. Your child's teachers will discuss his or her performance in each subject with you, including their targets and predicted grades.

Parents' evening is an opportunity to find out your child's targets from their teachers. If you feel your child is not where he or she is supposed to be, ask the teacher to advise on what you can do to help your child and to suggest resources that may help. Ask the teacher to tell you exactly how well or not your child is doing. Do not be satisfied with the usual default answer of "everything is finc" or "she is doing well". If time does not permit you to ask all the questions you have, arrange another time to meet the teacher. Teachers should be willing to meet parents to discuss their children's progress.

Speak to your child's teacher

Apart from parents' evenings, make time to see your child's teacher. Enquire about your child's performance in class and if there are any areas of concern. Most teachers are very encouraged when they notice that parents have an interest in their children's school work. Most primary schools keep their pupils' books in the school; make sure you check your child's workbook and note books if they are available on that day.

If you have a concern that your child is not being challenged enough, discuss this with the teacher. If you receive a bad report about your child from a teacher, discuss this with the teacher and investigate it fully to know the truth. If you are invited to the school to see the teacher, ask any questions calmly and be prepared to listen to the teacher's side. Do not immediately start disputing the teacher's claim without hearing what they have to say.

13. Employ a private tutor, if necessary

Not everybody is inclined to teach or support their children academically, and it is always possible that a time will come when you may not have enough knowledge to help your child with his or her academic work. See Chapter 8 for information on how to recognise a good tutor.

14. Invest in the best resources for your child

In the past, UK schools provided test books and digital resources for their students, but the current economic recession has led to the government cutting funds for schools. As a result of this, many schools have stopped supplying books to students and have also cancelled some external learning portals. However, parents can support their children by subscribing to education internet sites (such as MyMaths and MathsWatch) and buying useful books and DVDs.

15. Check his or her planner before signing it on weekly basis

Teachers write in their students' planners so that parents can be aware of what their children are doing in school, commenting on issues such as behaviour and attitude, lateness to the classroom, improper dress, and merits for good performance. Address these with your children. Give praise and encouragement for good merits, and discuss negative feedback and how they can be remedied or avoided in future.

16. Praise and reward your child

Most parents talk more about their children's poor performance than their good. Children should be rewarded for their good performance and encouraged to improve in the areas where they are not doing so well. One of the things I learned during my teacher training is how to give feedback to children. Start with a positive comment then point out the negatives, finishing with a word of encouragement. It is very important to acknowledge what they have done well before criticising them for things that need improvement.

17. Support them doing extracurricular activities

Encourage your child to do things outside of school that are not academic, like music, drama, dance, and sports. Attending their performances will encourage them and boost their self-esteem. Children are always proud to have their parents come to watch them perform. This also develops other skills outside the classroom. According to a medical website, www.medicaldaily.com, "people who play music not only have higher IQs but also have better problem solving and multitasking skills than people who do not play."

Jessica Hullinger in her writing, "11 problems music can solve," stated that a 2009 study comparing two groups of second graders from similar demographics suggests learning music boosts reading abilities. The only major difference between the two groups was that one learned music notation, sight-reading, and other skills, while the control group did not. Each group was tested for literacy before and after the school year. The end-of-year scores for the control group improved only slightly from their beginning of the year scores, while the kids with a music education scored "significantly higher", especially on vocabulary tests.[7]

A professional footballer turned teacher, Ben Burgess, transferred the skills he gained as a professional footballer into the classroom when he became a secondary school teacher. He wrote on the BBC sport website that:

"To play professional football you need to have more skills and strengths than people give us credit for. Determination, leadership skills, ability to work in a team, performance under pressure, focus and

[7] Jessica Hullinger "11 problems music can solve", mentalfloss.com

adaptability... just some of the unique skills we all possess that are transferable to the outside world. What employer would not want an employee with those credentials on their CV?"[8]

18. Ask your child about his or her school day

It is important to know what is going on with your child at school. You need to choose the right time to ask as some children may not want to discuss this, especially if something is wrong or they are feeling upset or guilty about something. Ask about the work they have done that day, what they ate, who they played with, and if there was any trouble at school. Expect them to answer you with, "It's alright," or, "It was fine," or, "Everything was okay." You need to be very gentle and inquisitive to get the truth from them. Another common answer is, "Kind of." Go further in

[8] Ben Burgess: Ex-Blackpool and Hull striker on becoming a teacher, http://www.bbc.co.uk/sport/0/football/29972022

asking questions, otherwise you will not know what is going on. Your interaction with your child will alert you to issues such as bullying, problems with teachers, problems with school work, or general unhappiness in school.

19. Speak positive words into a child's life, and pray for your child

Negative words used by parents have a profound effect on children's self-esteem, while positive words boost their ego and confidence. Positive words with patience will change many children's lives.

Prayers play a major role in our children's lives. We have seen a lot of changes in their lives as result of prayer, and I encourage every parent to create time to pray for their children.

20. Do not give up on your child

Two parents shared testimonies of their two young adults who are at university with me recently. These two young adults gave their parents a difficult time when they were in secondary school but their parents continued to support them, provided private tutoring for them, spoke words of encouragement to them, and often prayed for them. It was very tough but they did not give up on them. They did well at the end of their sixth form, got into universities, saw life from another context and dimension, became "born again" (not in a religious context), and now appreciate their parents' support, especially for not giving up on them. I am extracting one of the testimonies from our Facebook education group page:

"We are all doing fine to the Glory of God. She is back for her second year. She is doing really well as

you said we should not give up on our children at all. She has a 2.1 for her first year already. Thanks for your support and words of encouragement oh, oh, she is finding so much joy in the course, yes oh pastor she is doing very well and she has really changed a lot now looking forward to coming home and going to church with us every
Sunday. God is really good."

That can be your story if you do not give up on your child.

CHAPTER 8
Choosing a Private Tutor

Many parents have been disappointed with the private tutors who prepare their children for different exams. However, the academic success of a child is not solely dependent on tutors or teachers; parents also have a major role to play. It is the duty of parents to do proper research before employing private tutors for their children. Do not be deceived or carried away by the 100% pass rate claimed by many tutors. Rely more on recommendations from other parents. The cost of private tuition varies considerably between tutors.

Consider the average cost of private tuition in your area when making your decision. In my opinion, a good tutor must have the following:

1. The knowledge and experience of teaching or tutoring the subject in question.
2. If it is for the Eleven Plus exam, the knowledge of the selection process of the council or school administering the exam.
3. A passion to teach or tutor a child of that exam age.
4. A good track record of pass rates and, preferably, a record of tutees who have attended your school of choice.
5. Good organisational and time management skills.
6. Effective communication skills.
7. An approachable nature.

8. Time set aside to feedback on the child they are tutoring.

9. Registration with the Disclosure and Barring Service (DBS), formerly the Criminal Records Bureau (CRB).

CHAPTER 9

Are There State Boarding Schools in the UK?

Yes, there are state boarding schools in the UK. Boarding schools are not limited to private schools; some state-maintained schools (both grammar and comprehensive schools) also have boarding facilities. Although students attend the school for free, parents have to pay for boarding and other related fees. As with the private boarding schools, some state-maintained boarding schools operate weekday boarding facilities (where students go back home for the weekend) and others operate full boarding facilities (where students go home only during half-term breaks and holidays). You can find more information about state maintained boarding schools on the SBSA (State Boarding Schools Association) website (http://www.sbsa.org.uk/). As a state-funded school, it is only available to children permanently residing in the UK.

CHAPTER 10

Funding Your Child's Secondary Education in a State Maintained Secondary School

State schools (also known as Government or State Maintained Schools) are funded by the state government, but schools normally ask for a voluntary contribution from parents on a monthly or yearly basis. The amount of this voluntary contribution depends on the individual school. Since it is 'voluntary', schools are not expected to put pressure on parents to contribute, but some do.

However, it is the responsibility of parents to pay for school trips, music lessons, sports kits, and school uniforms. Parents who cannot afford to pay for these extras may be eligible for help if they meet certain criteria. Schools may be able to assist parents who cannot afford to pay for their children's school trips, and the local council may be able to assist with the cost of school meals, uniforms, music lessons, and transportation costs (from home to school).

Some private organisations award music or general grants to high-ability pupils from low-income families. More information is available on the website (http://www.turn2us.org.uk/). You can also check the internet.

CHAPTER 11

Independence Secondary School Transfer

The private schools' admission process is outside the State system. You need to apply to an individual private school, which normally costs a fee.

Common entrance into a private secondary school is almost the same as with state-funded schools, except that the test is administered by an organisation known as the Independent Schools Examination Board (ISEB) for some private schools, followed by an interview process and references from your child's present head teacher. Some private secondary schools admit students into Year 7 immediately after Year 6 while some only admit students into Year 9 when the children are 13 plus. Some private schools are boarding schools while some are day schools and some are a mixture of the two. Most of the private schools are divided into a Junior Secondary School and a Senior Secondary School. The Junior Secondary is Years 7 and 8 while the Senior Secondary is Years 9-11 and Sixth Form.

Some private schools operate a two-tiered admission test system. The first entrance examination or test take place in November. Successful students will be selected for the second entrance test in January. The preparation is the same as for the Eleven Plus. The most important thing is that you need to find out the subjects your child will be tested on and start the preparation early. For Eleven Plus Common Entrance, most private schools test students on maths, English, verbal reasoning (VR), and non-verbal reasoning (NVR). The Thirteen Plus entrance examination takes place when children are in Year 8; the test is based on what they would have studied in Years 7 and 8. Some private school tests focus only on maths, English, and science, while others will test other Year 8 subjects in addition to these (especially for children who are attending a private school already, known as prep school but are joining another private school in Year 9). It is very important that you check with the school you want your child to attend.

Checking the school's academic performance is also very important. According to my research, there are some state-funded schools in the UK that outperform some private schools at GCSE and A Levels but most top private schools are academically stronger than state-funded schools and it is not a secret that private schools have very high intakes in our top universities as well. They also dominate most of the higher professions and government in the UK. You also need to check the private school to see if it is suitable for your child. I know a few parents who sent their children to private primary schools but then sent them to state-funded secondary schools. I also know a few parents whose children took their GCSEs at a private school but moved to a state-funded secondary school for the Sixth Form. I am also aware of children who moved to private schools in Year 9 and Year 12 from state-funded schools.

Private schools do have their advantages over state-funded schools, especially with extracurricular activities such as sport, drama, character building, and holistic education.

Guardians in the UK

Children attending private boarding schools in the UK from other countries are expected to have a guardian residing in the country. This can be a family member or a professional guardian. Professional guardians are people who deputise for parents if their child is in a UK private school on a financial basis. This means parents are paying for his or her services. Guardians are required for overseas students in the UK in case of emergencies, or during short holidays when everybody has to leave the school boarding house.

CHAPTER 12

Private School Funding

All private schools are fee-paying schools, but financial assistance can be provided to parents through scholarships and bursaries. Some private schools offer discounts if fees are paid early and if parents have more than one child in the school.

What is the difference between a scholarship and a bursary?

A scholarship is financial assistance or support given to a student based on academic, sport, music, art, or drama achievements. This is irrespective of parents' income. Most private schools offer academic scholarships to students based on their performance in the Common Entrance Examination test. In some private schools, parents have to apply for their children to sit for the scholarship test. The value of the scholarship varies from school to school but is usually not more than 50 percent of the total tuition fees.

A bursary is means-tested financial assistance given to parents who otherwise cannot afford to pay the school fees. Means-tested financial assistance is based on both parents' disposable income. A bursary is sometimes used to supplement a scholarship, and this could be up to 100% of the school fee. Most schools review their bursaries every year, while a scholarship usually covers the child for the duration of their study in that school. If you want your child to attend a private school, it is very important to contact the school early for information on financial assistance. Some organisations, such as "Turn to Us" and many others offer educational grants to children attending independent schools based on meeting some criteria.

Even if the school offers your child a scholarship and/or a bursary, you will still have to cover some expenses known as extra or options. The private school will be able to provide information on what these extras are. There are some independents that do not have scholarship or bursary facilities so inquire with the school before applying if you cannot afford school fee.

CHAPTER 13

Sixth Form

Sixth Form is the bridge between secondary school and university. It is commonly known as 'A Levels'. Sixth Form is the last two years of secondary school before Further or Advanced Education and it is also known as Key Stage 5 in the national curriculum structure. Not all secondary schools, especially comprehensive schools, have an integral Sixth Form, hence, students who attend schools without Sixth Form have to apply to other secondary schools with integral Sixth Form or a Sixth Form College. Sixth Form is not compulsory in the UK as the compulsory school age stops at 16, while Sixth Form is for pupils aged 6-18, but they can go to colleges to obtain vocational qualifications for access to university education.

Presently, Sixth Form offers GCSE "A" Level, while some do offer International Baccalaureate (IB) and others offer both. In addition to these two qualifications, some private schools offer some qualifications known as the International General School Certificate of Education (IGSCE) and PreU. Students have to choose any of the qualifications if they are attending schools that offer more than one of these qualifications.

Debates have been going on for some time about which of the two is better between IB and A levels for students. IB has more subjects to be studied than A level and it allows students to continue studying the core subjects of maths, English, and science throughout their Sixth Form. Many articles have been written on these two Sixth Form qualifications; I advise parents to search for them on the internet and make their own decisions.

Admission into Sixth Form is similar to applying for Year 7 after primary school. This starts with open days in November before the entry year. Parents visit schools offering Sixth Form with their children, see their resources, attend the head teacher's talk and have an opportunity to ask current students about their experiences in the school. They also have the opportunity to ask teachers questions as well but remember that nobody will say anything bad about his or her school.

Students can apply to more than one Sixth Form school and college, including his or her current school's Sixth Form if it has one. Some leading grammar schools will ask students to take a test on the subjects they intend to study in Sixth Form or take a test in maths if they want to take it as part of their course. Sixth Form offers provisional admission to students based on their predicted grades and is finalised after submission of their GCSE results if they fulfil the required grades.

It is very important for students who want to attend a leading Sixth Form school or college to know that their predicted grades will determine their offers into these schools; therefore, they need to work hard while they are in Year 9 and 10 and prepare for their mock exams in Year 11 as if they are preparing for their final GCSE exam. As I normally tell students, their predicted grades and GCSEs will play a major role in their Sixth Form admission and their "AS" result, and "A2" with teachers' predicted grades will play a major role in their university's admission, so they have to work hard from the beginning and not wait for mock time before preparing. I read in the newspaper that most leading universities do not go to clearing (clearing is how universities fill places left on their courses after the initial offers and allocations) as they would have enough students to fill their courses before clearing, which is after the A level results have been published.

Recently, the government abolished the national exam after the first year known as 'AS'. The effect of this is that most universities without an entrance test will base their conditional admission on a student's GCSE result, predicted grade, competitive personal statement, school reference, and interview, if there is one. My advice to students is that they should work very hard with their GCSEs if they want to attend a leading or top performing university.

Hard work does not kill, but rewards you with good success.

GRAMMAR SCHOOL OR ANY OTHER SCHOOL DOES NOT MAKE A CHILD. YOUR CHILD WILL EXCEL ANYWHERE IF GIVEN THE RIGHT SUPPORT BY PARENTS.

CHAPTER 14

Is Failing the Eleven Plus Test the End of the World?

Children who fail the Eleven Plus test can attempt the Twelve Plus and Thirteen Plus tests. If they are still unable to pass these, rest assured it is not the end of the world. A student can still gain entry into a leading university and have a good career in life even if he or she does not attend a private school or grammar school, provided there is continued support from their parents. It does not matter whether your child attends a private school, grammar school, or comprehensive school; the most important things are academic achievement, passion, and leadership skills. As an organisation, Kingsgen Academy and Kingsgen Foundation are working hard to achieve these major life skills with all our tutees and mentees. Independent schools and grammar schools provide a better learning environment for their students, but students with parental support and a good attitude to learning do achieve and excel in life without attending a private school. Like a single parent of four achieving young adults wrote in the newspaper some years ago, "It is not where you are but who you are." I will end this book by saying geographical location should not define, limit or determine who you will be in life. There are many opportunities for our children, but they're very competitive. Help to unearth the treasure in them and bring out the genius in them. Our children are stars, they all carry the seed of greatness; help to water and prune it and it will surely bare fruits. As the saying goes, "Your attitude will determine your altitude."

Join us to raise the next generation of achievers and transformation leaders over the world. We can start now to make a difference and leave a good legacy for our children.

APPENDIX 1

While writing this book, the government has changed the Secondary school GCSE grading system from alphabetical grades (e.g. A*, A, and B) to numerical grades (e.g. 9-8, 7, and 6). The new grading system will be effective from 2017, but some schools will use it for their in-house assessment in parallel to the present grading system. This new grading system starts in summer 2017 for English, maths, and science.

The secondary school grading system

OLD GCSE grading system	NEW GCSE grading system
A*	9-8
A	7
B	6
C	5/4
D	4
E	3
F	2
G	1
U	U

APPENDIX 2

Parents' Testimonials

These are a few testimonials from much feedback we received from parents who have attended our seminars or whom we have worked with and with their children:

"One thing that makes me fall in love with Pastor Nick is that he has great passion to make contributions to the world of our children so that they are positioned to achieve their potentials and is always searching for means to ensure this passion is realised. He has navigated, in no small means, my children in gaining admission in to grammar school. This is the best that can happen to anyone. He always believes that there is no child without potential and he perceives this in all children who comes his way. More importantly, he relies on the leading of the spirit. Please keep it up, the sky cannot limit you." Mr. Dele Oyedele (Welling)

"My family and I relocated from Atlanta, Georgia about a year ago. Our first daughter was going to start preparations for Eleven Plus exams. We had contacted a tutoring agency in London from Atlanta but we did not get a prompt response from them. Hence, we were desperate to start with the preparations and we only had about nine weeks to prepare. On a visit to one of our friends, we were referred to Pastor Nick. We immediately got in touch with Pastor Nick and our journey of Eleven Plus started. As we made our first visit to Pastor Nick's home in Dartford his passion, enthusiasm, and positive attitude were evident. He immediately guided us on how to complete all the forms for the exams. He strongly suggested that we enter our daughter for Kent, Medway, and Bexley. On that same day, he accompanied us with his car and we submitted two of the forms so as to meet the deadlines. What efficiency and dedication, you will agree!! Pastor Nick was very honest with us that we were starting late but that if our daughter would pass the exam if she worked hard. At that first meeting, he diligently acquainted us with his standards and work ethos and that of the exam board. We knew exactly what we had to do.

Furthermore, Pastor Nick believed so much in our daughter and he was very interested in her success. In addition, he was very considerate and worked patiently around our rather tight schedule. He helped us create a healthy balance and continuously looked for better and more effective techniques and resources needed to help our daughter succeed.

Throughout the preparation, Pastor Nick tutored our daughter, provided resources, and supported her with prayers and encouragement. He was a tutor, coach, and facilitator. Our daughter was motivated and worked at least four hours daily, including weekends in the summer of 2010. In September, she took all three exams. We are grateful to God and to Pastor Nick and happy to say that our daughter passed all the three Eleven Plus exams and in fact scored the highest in her school in the Medway Eleven Plus exams. She will be starting at Rochester Grammar school in September. We will always recommend Pastor Nick to families who need strong support as they navigate this area of their child's education. Thank you." Tosin and Leke Oteju

“I met you two weeks before my son was due to do the grammar test. It was difficult to believe that you could prepare someone in such a short time. However, the materials, your dedication, and belief that Mike could do it meant I trusted you. It made it much easier because my son wanted to go to grammar school and needed someone who could believe in him so that’s how he was able to achieve so much. What was also touching was your nurturing and taking the time to speak to him before he sat the exam. I felt that it was impressive and I can only again say thank you.” Hyacinthe (Welling)

“Thank you for putting the programme together and God bless all your efforts. I found it very informative on the following levels:

- Knowing that as a parent I have responsibility in investing my time and effort into my children's futures to allow them to fulfil their destinies
- Knowing that there are available resources out there I can utilise
- Knowing what to do from an early stage with my children and not wait till the last minute
- Knowing the different types of schools and a bit on how to access them (in the future it would be good to go into more detail)
- Your guest speaker was very informative and delivered his talk effectively (I took nearly two pages of notes)
- I liked the way you backed up what you were saying with evidence (clips and people in the audience)

- Thank you for the refreshments: they were nice and it was good to have fruit as well
- You are well researched and evidently know what you are talking about because you live and breathe it. Your passion for education was very evident and you wanted to share this with us in the short time available. It would have been nice to explore particular areas in more depth.
- I am very pleased that I took up the offer and will be taking up other offers and inviting others as well.
- The question and answer time was a brilliant idea." Mrs. Lara Amusan (Belvedere, Kent)

"It was a great pleasure to attend the 'Building Your Children's Future' seminar on Saturday. I was very blessed and found the seminar very practical and straight to the point. I learnt about the types of schools in the UK and the importance of getting involved as a parent in my children's education. I was very blessed by the talk from the deputy head teacher and alas I have been praying Daniel 1:4 over my children since Saturday and do not intend to stop. I am so excited about it that I have being telling my friends who missed it to get ready for the next seminar." Mrs. Bukkie Mogaji (Chatham Kent)

"Yes, it was beneficial in the sense that my son now knows that what we have being doing and are still doing is for his own good. Most of what your guest shared is exactly what we have in place and, when our son was relating it back to his dad, he simply said, 'That is what you guys are doing.' Thanks and God bless you and your house abundantly." Mrs. Pauline Sowemimo (Sutton)

"Thank you too, it was time well spent. Thank you for divulging such first-hand information to us. It was quite beneficial and I am sure it will come in handy in the near future." Mrs. Renie Hardas (Stockwell)

"My experience of the evening was really inspirational. Of late, I have become really concerned about my children's education, and how I can best support them. I am relieved that there are like-minded people who are willing to share their experience and support other families in getting the best for their children. I look forward to moving on with the programme and seeing my son get more excited about his school work. Thank you, Pastor and Mrs Nunayon." Mrs. Gilka M (Stockwell)

"Travelling all the way from Chafford Hundred, Essex to Dulwich, South East London for this seminar worth every second of it. I gained a lot and look forward to the next one." Mrs. Lara Odunsi (Essex)

"Firstly, I wish to commend you for your passion and zeal with respect to the subject matter. I was personally impressed with your level of confidence and knowledge on the subject.
Coming to the seminar made me understand that:

1. My current frustrations are not unfounded

2. I am not alone

3. There is a sure way out

The seminar also gave me a sneak peek into the current school system and specifically at the low levels of achievement which the government has set as a standard for schools." Mrs Ruth A (Wallington)

"I was greatly inspired by events on Saturday. I wish more people would wake up to the things you were saying." Pastor Adebayo Ademiju (Essex)

"May the Lord continually bless your tireless efforts and crown it all with success beyond what you can even begin to imagine, IJN. The seminar was indeed an eye opener. Parents' contributions were also a big positive." Mrs. Lara Lawson (Surrey)

"When is the next seminar? Your seminars really blessed me and opened my eyes to new things I was not aware of at all, so thanks lots." Mrs. Toyin Thompson (Lambeth London)

"I bless God for your life, sir. For all your supports, prayers, encouragement, and tireless motivation. You are indeed a father, brother, mentor, teacher, motivator, and a destiny helper. May the good Lord reward you abundantly, both here on earth and in heaven and bless your hard work. Our God is indeed an awesome God. God is indeed glorious and all sufficient. I thank God for all at Kingsgen. May the grace, mercy, favour, and anointing of God rest and abide with us all in Jesus' name. We love you all." Faith and Diana Ibrahim

You can read more testimonials on our websites

Kingsgen.co.uk

Kingsgenacademy.org

Important Websites

BBC Educational News website

http://www.bbc.co.uk/news/education-30633305

Help with school subjects and resources

www.bbc.co.uk/education

www.mathsisfun.com

www.parentsintouch.co.uk

www.youtube.com

QUOTES ON EDUCATION

"You educate a man; you educate a man. You educate a woman; you educate a generation."

Brigham Young

"Education is the most powerful weapon which you can use to change the world."

Nelson Mandela

"Whatever the cost of our libraries, the price is cheap compared to that of an ignorant nation."

Walter Cronkite

"Children must be taught how to think, not what to think."

Margaret Mead

"Give a girl an education and introduce her properly into the world, and ten to one but she has the means of settling well, without further expense to anybody."

Jane Austen

"Education without values, as useful as it is, seems rather to make man a more clever devil."

C.S. Lewis

"Educate a boy, and you educate an individual.

Educate a girl, and you educate a community."

Adelaide Hoodless

Kingsgen Academy
(Building Our Children's Future)
Register your child now for:
11plus, 12plus & 13plus preparations
All our tutors are CRB checked
Also for:
• Year 3, 4 and 5 tuition and support
• Year 6 SAT Preparations
• Year 7-11 Maths, English and Science Support including GCSE preparations
• Independent Secondary Schools entrance examinations preparations
" A Supplementary School with a Very High Pass rate"
Registration hotline: 07735480007 07985423504
Venue: St Catherine's Catholic School
Watling Street, Bexleyheath, Kent, DA6 7QJ
admin@kingsgen.co.uk • www.kingsgen.co.uk • kingsgenacademy@gmail.com • www.kingsgenacademy.co.uk

For your educational needs, consultancy, seminars, coaching, mentoring, and workshops in your churches, charity organisations, youth clubs, and so on

Contact us on 07735480007

Email me: nicknunayon@hotmail.com

Visit our website www.kingsgen.co.uk

www.kingsgenacademy.org